3D PAPER CRAFTS
for Kids

For a printable PDF of the templates used in this book, please contact Fox Chapel Publishing at customerservice@foxchapelpublishing.com, stating the ISBN and title of the book in the subject line.

All photos and illustrations by the author unless otherwise noted. The following images are credited to Shutterstock.com and their respective creators: girl (back cover): Dragon Images; scissors (pages 3, 4, and front and back cover): akiyoko; shapes (page 4 and front cover): Blan-k; crafting background (page 95): Arina P Habich; squiggly lines (throughout): Yevgenij_D; wavy lines (throughout): Meranna

ISBN 978-1-64124-117-5

Library of Congress Control Number: 2021935130

To learn more about the other great books from Fox Chapel Publishing, or to find a retailer near you, call toll-free 800-457-9112 or visit us at *www.FoxChapelPublishing.com*.

We are always looking for talented authors. To submit an idea, please send a brief inquiry to acquisitions@foxchapelpublishing.com.

Fox Chapel Publishing makes every effort to use environmentally friendly paper for printing.

Printed in China
Second printing

3D PAPER CRAFTS

for Kids

26 Creative Projects to Make from A–Z

HELEN DREW
of Arty Crafty Kids

Happy Fox
BOOKS

CONTENTS

30

18

24

34

48

28

22

26

56

62

42

20

60

Introduction

Welcome to *3D Paper Crafts for Kids*, your ultimate guide to learning through play.

As well as bringing you lots of arty inspiration and craft ideas for all occasions, this book—and all the activities inside it—can be used to explore the alphabet, to spark children's curiosity, and to make learning fun.

Just pick a letter and dive in!

At Arty Crafty Kids, we believe in the power of creativity and, as parents ourselves, we have seen firsthand the benefits that come from engaging children in interactive crafts. From building confidence and fostering self-expression, to encouraging a love of learning, to introducing mindfulness, there's so much for children to discover though dynamic and hands-on crafting. Three-dimensional paper crafts are a wonderfully simple but effective way to engage children of all ages and nurture those benefits.

Our A–Z book of crafts introduces children to 3D effects using simple techniques like folds, accordions, and paper loops. The extra dimension encourages children to explore the ideas of perspective, depth, and movement in a really easy-to-understand way that offers lots of opportunity for discussion. These crafts are also more effective than basic crafts or coloring at helping to hone fine motor skills.

To complement our crafts' tactile nature, many of our projects incorporate art techniques that really enhance each project—ones that can be scaled up or down depending on the age of your child. We've found this to be a truly winning combination, resulting in a full creative experience that is guaranteed to spark an interest in art that will last a lifetime.

Although colored pencils and markers are absolutely fine (especially for little ones!), we often use paint instead, which presents a world of exciting opportunities for children. They can experiment with color mixing to create new shades, refine their work with blending, learn more about color theory, and explore pattern and texture with techniques like splattering. They can even discover that there's more than one way to use a paintbrush!

But learning is just one part of it—we're also big believers in bringing play into craft. Our 3D crafts are so tactile, the whole process of creating them is engaging and fun—and when the craft is finished, it's only the beginning! Children can carry on the fun, whether it's reimagining different animals and playing with perspective, or wiggling and jiggling away with a 3D bobblehead craft.

We hope that your children enjoy this compilation of our best 3D paper crafts just as much as we enjoyed developing them.

Helen
x

—Helen and the Arty Crafty Kids team

Common Paper Folding Techniques

Throughout this book, children will have the opportunity to hone their fine motor skills and master a variety of paper folding techniques to create 3D effects. Each of these paper folds will help to enhance and lift different elements of the craft, adding a sense of perspective, dimension, and, in some projects, movement. The paper strips needed for these techniques can be created using scissors and a ruler, or, if you have one, a paper cutter.

Loop

This simple technique will be used frequently to create small lifts.

Step 1. Start with a strip of paper. Use a long piece for a large loop and a short one for a tight, small loop.

Glue the ends together here.

Step 2. Gently bend the paper around so that the two ends meet and create a circle, but don't fold or crease the paper.

Step 3. Secure the ends together with glue to make a closed loop.

Zigzag

Zigzags are great for larger lifts with lots of bounce.

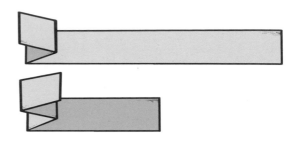

Step 1. Start with a long strip of paper.

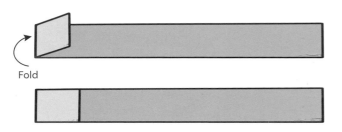

Step 2. Fold one end of the strip (just a short piece, about as long as the strip is wide) on top of itself, and press it down to create a crease.

Step 3. Take the same end of the strip and make a second fold, this time to the back side instead of to the front side, making the new fold the same size as your first flap. Press to crease. (Alternatively, you can flip the strip to the other side and simply repeat the very first flap fold to the front.) Viewing the strip from the side, you will notice a triangular shape. This is the start of the zigzag formation.

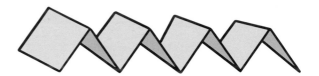

Step 4. Continue the process of folding forward and backward (or forward, flipping, and forward again) along the whole strip of paper.

Accordion

This springy little fold will add a lot of lift in a more stable, solid manner than a zigzag.

Step 1. Cut two strips of paper of equal size.

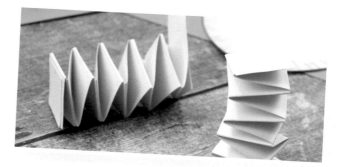

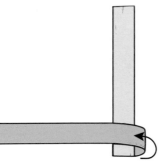

Step 2. Glue the ends of the paper strips together, overlapping to form a right angle, with the vertical paper on top.

Glue under here!

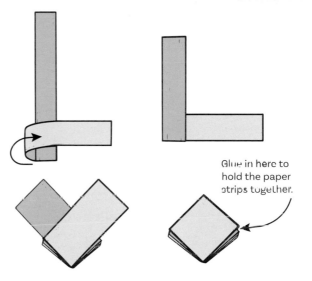

Glue in here to hold the paper strips together.

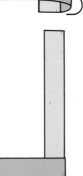

Step 3. Tightly fold the bottom paper strip back over the top one.

Step 4. Now fold the paper strip that is now on the bottom back over the top one again. Continue this pattern, always folding the bottom strip on top of the other strip, until you have folded all the way to the end and are left with a neat little square. Trim any extra off the ends, then secure the top end with glue.

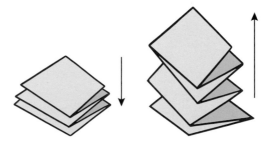

Step 5. With both ends secure, pull open the folds to reveal the accordion.

Curl

Curls are a great way to add dimension and texture in the form of hair or other features.

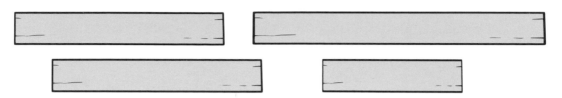

Step 1. Start with a strip of paper. The paper can be short or long, wide or thin.

Step 2. Roll the paper tightly around a pencil or paintbrush.

Step 3. Carefully slide the paper roll off the pencil or paintbrush. Allow the roll to naturally unravel. If necessary, help it along until it's the size you want.

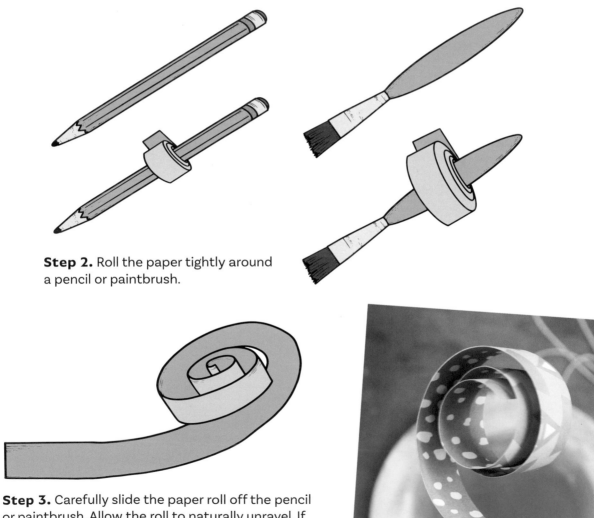

Finding and Organizing Materials

The Whole World's a Treasure Trove

Before we delve into organizing an art cart, we should discuss its materials. The craft store is likely to be the first choice for accumulating a base collection of materials such as paper, cardstock, pipe cleaners, pom-poms, and the like, but an amazing variety of free and wondrous resources can also be found within the home and outdoors.

How often do your children return from a nature walk with pockets full of stones, sticks, or other special treasures? All of these items can be repurposed, and children will find great delight in using them!

My own children love rummaging through the recycling bin, too, for it presents a plethora of materials of random shapes and textures, all of which can be reimagined into a special project. Additionally, old clothes with their buttons, zippers, embellishments, and differing fabrics present all sorts of upcycling and creative opportunities. With a little imagination, children have the capability to transform anything into something new. When you look around, you'll find that a treasure trove of craft materials is readily available.

The Magic of an Art Cart

In my experience, an art cart is one of the best ways to organize a wide array of purchased and recycled materials. They are portable, space saving (storing everything in one place!), and help to foster a sense of creative freedom. When children are able to freely explore materials, they are given an opportunity to use their imaginations to expand and discover their creativity.

You can purchase various accessories to enhance an art cart's storage capabilities, from extra pots that hang from the side to ribbon organizers and neat divider trays that rest on top of any level. Pom-poms, googly eyes, craft sticks, and more can be stored within the cart using a tray, plastic tubs, or recycled jars. All of these organizational tricks feed into one key objective: to make crafting with children accessible, easy, and fun.

To keep the art cart fresh and exciting, you should make it a practice to rotate materials. Always keep paint, pencils, scissors, markers, and glue readily available. However, the unusual may include a pot of salt (great for raised salt painting), an array of natural materials, recyclable materials of all different shapes, sizes, and textures, and some variety in artistic mediums, from chalk pastels to empty bottles for spray art. Simple rotation will keep children engaged and curious in their arty, crafty adventures.

Apples

An apple craft a day keeps the boredom at bay! Children's fine motor skills and concentration will both get a workout with this craft as they build up their spheres, loop by loop, to create an overflowing basket of fruit. Whether they're learning about the fall season or about healthy eating, kids will love this fun and bright apple activity.

MATERIALS

- Template (page 64)
- Yellow, red, green, brown, and various other colors of paint
- 4 paper strips each in yellow, red, and green
- Green tissue paper
- Craft straw
- Scissors
- Glue stick
- Paintbrush

1. Paint the apples. Paint or color in the basket and apples template, making one apple yellow, one red, and one green.

2. Glue the first strip. Find the matching paper strips for one colored apple. Gently fold each end of the first paper strip and apply glue to the folded-over areas. Secure one glued area to one edge of the apple circle and then gently bend the paper strip across the circle to its opposite edge to create an arch. Secure the other end here.

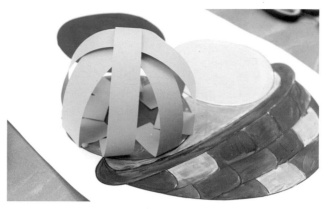

3. Glue the second strip. Repeat with a second strip of the same color to create an "X" across the circle.

4. Finish the apple. Fill in the remaining gaps with two more strips of paper—a cross on top of the existing "X"—to create a beautifully rounded apple.

5. Glue the other apples. Create two more apples using the remaining strips of paper, matching the strip colors to each apple again.

6. Add straw. Add a layer of glue to the inside of the basket and fill the area with cut-up craft straw.

7. Add leaves. Cut out several leaf shapes from green tissue paper and attach at least one to each apple.

Butterfly

Discover the transformational beauty of the butterfly with this colorful craft. Children can explore symmetry, printing, and pattern-making through this simple but engaging activity that's impressive enough to be hung up once complete—the perfect decoration for any classroom or playroom.

MATERIALS

- Favorite coloring medium (such as paint, crayons, or paint sticks)
- White cardstock
- Pipe cleaner
- A round object, e.g., a jar lid (optional)
- Scissors

Paper Folding Technique: Zigzag

1. Make a colorful drawing. Create an arty masterpiece on a sheet of white cardstock. You'll need one sheet per butterfly. Then cut the artwork into two segments: a square and rectangle. (These don't need to be exact—just make sure one is larger than the other, as shown.)

2. Round the corners. Use scissors to round off all the corners of both cut shapes. You can do this freehand or by tracing the edge of a round object first.

3. Fold the shapes. Next, fold each shape in the zigzag fold, starting from the longest edge. Try to keep the folds nice and even.

4. Fold in half. Squeeze the folds in your hand to create a strip. Fold this strip in half one way and again in the other direction. Repeat with the other folded shape.

5. Tie together. Place the folded square strip on top of the folded rectangle strip and secure the two pieces together by wrapping a pipe cleaner around the middle of both.

6. Make the antennae. Wrap the pipe cleaner two or three more times around the paper strips and secure with a twist. There should be enough pipe cleaner remaining for you to create the appearance of antennae—if not, unwrap part of the pipe cleaner.

7. Spread the wings. Once the pipe cleaner is firmly in place, open up the folds and spread out the butterfly's wings.

Cat

Cats have a majestic presence and heaps of personality, so they're a great animal to explore with art and crafts. Children can undertake their own little cat character study with this fun 3D activity and play with color, fur markings, and different ways of expressing personality. Will their cat be politely waiting for dinner or cheekily ready to pounce?

MATERIALS

- Template (page 65)
- Favorite coloring medium (such as paint, crayons, or paint sticks)
- Any color backing cardstock

- 3 black cardstock strips
- Black and/or white markers
- Scissors
- Glue stick

Paper Folding Techniques:
Loop
Accordion
Zigzag

1. Color and cut out the cat. Paint or color in the template. Consider giving it spots, splats, or stripes—or maybe it will be rainbow, all black, white, or orange with bright piercing eyes. Once your cat is dry, carefully cut out each individual cat element.

2. Finish the face. Assemble the cat's head, adding two ears, two eyes, and a nose. Using a black marker (or a white one, depending on the color of the cat), draw whiskers and a mouth.

3. Add the paws. Take one paper strip and cut it in half. Create two paper loops with these short strips. For guidance, place the cat's head or body near the bottom of the backing cardstock, then secure a paper loop on either side of the head or body. Add a paw to the top of each loop.

4. Attach the tail. Now it's time to make a decision: will your cat be a pouncer or a sitter? Ours will become a pouncer! That means the head will be at the bottom and the body up top. Add a kink to the tail by adding a slight zigzag fold to it, and then affix the tail to the cat's bottom.

5. Attach the body. Glue the cat's body to the backing cardstock, allowing the tail to slightly overhang the edge of the cardstock.

6. Attach the head. Next, use two paper strips to make an accordion. Glue it just below the cat's body, then affix the cat's head on top. Our feline friend's head will now wiggle and wobble in preparation to pounce! If you're making a sitting cat instead, place the head above the body. Give it an inquisitive tilt if you like!

Duck

A trip to feed the ducks is a firm childhood favorite, so why not bring that joy into learning and play with this cute duck craft? Since the duck pieces are almost like a puzzle, children will enjoy figuring out how the different elements come together before they really bring it to life with a springy 3D wing—*quack!*

MATERIALS

- Template (pages 66 and 67)
- Favorite coloring medium (such as paint, crayons, or paint sticks)
- 4 yellow or brown construction paper strips
- Scissors
- Glue stick

1. Color and cut out the template. Paint or color in both pages of the template. Carefully cut out all the elements.

2. Make the head. Assemble the head by adding a beak, an eye, and a rosy cheek to the smaller circle.

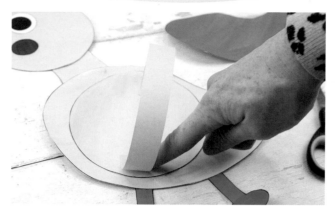

3. Assemble the body. Glue the head and neck together and attach it to the duck's body. Add the duck's feet to the lower body. Glue the second circle within the body. This will become the base and guide for the duck's pot-belly.

4. Glue the first strip. Gently fold each end of one paper strip and apply glue to the folded-over areas. Secure one glued area to one edge of the circle and then gently bend the paper strip across the circle to its opposite edge to create an arch. Secure the other end here.

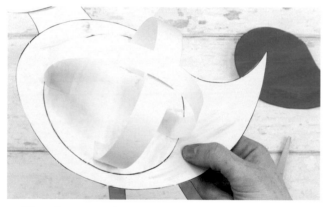

5. Glue the second strip. Repeat with a second strip to create an "X" across the tummy.

6. Finish the belly. Fill in the remaining gaps with two more strips of paper—a cross on top of the existing "X"—to complete the duck's pot-belly.

7. Add the wing. Glue the remaining wing element to the top of the pot-belly.

Elephant

If your kids have ever wanted to get up close and personal with an elephant, now's their chance! This fun activity is a great way for children to explore the elephant's oversized features as they use different paper craft techniques to create depth. With her flapping ears and bouncing trunk, this elephant is guaranteed to deliver hours of safari fun!

MATERIALS

- Template (pages 68 and 69)
- Any color backing cardstock (such as yellow)
- Gray and pink cardstock
- 6 gray cardstock strips, including one wider than the others

- Black marker
- Scissors
- Glue stick
- Pencil

Paper Folding Technique: Loop

1. Cut out the template. Carefully cut out all the elephant shapes from the template.

2. Trace and assemble. On gray cardstock, trace around the elephant's head, trunk, and larger ear shapes. On pink cardstock, trace around the smaller ear shapes. Cut out all the shapes. Glue the small pink ears onto the larger gray ones. Then glue the eyes onto the elephant's head.

3. Prep the ears. Fold the ears in half gently—don't create a firm crease, just fold enough so that the ears have some dimension. Then glue the inner side of each ear to the backing cardstock, leaving space in the middle for the head. Don't glue the whole ear down—we want them to flap from the page like Dumbo about to take off!

 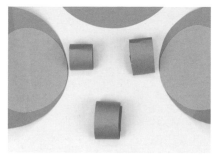 

4. Add ear loops. Create two small paper loops from gray strips of cardstock. Glue a loop under the outer edge of each ear to help lift them.

5. Add more loops. Make three more loops from gray strips. Glue one loop onto the backing cardstock next to each ear, then glue the third loop between the first two, but about an inch (a couple centimeters) down.

6. Attach the head. Carefully glue the elephant's head onto the three loops. Make sure you don't cover the back of the head with glue, otherwise your elephant might end up stuck to the background!

7. Make a big loop. Now we need to create a sixth loop, but this one needs to be bigger than the others, so use a wider strip of gray cardstock. Make a large loop and secure the ends. Then gently flatten it a little between your hands and glue it onto the elephant's head, right beneath the eyes.

8. Prep the trunk. Draw some black, slightly curved, horizontal lines with your marker down the length of the trunk to give it the creased look that elephants' trunks are known for. Then gently bend the trunk into an "S" shape. When you unbend it, it will be left with a perfect curve to flow over the 3D loop—no elephant's trunk is straight!

9. Attach the trunk. Glue the top half of the trunk onto the large paper loop and BOING— your elephant is done!

Fish

Explore all the color and movement of the deep blue sea with this swimmingly good paper fish craft. From stamping paint in order to build scales, to tearing cardstock in order to create waves of water, there are so many different ways for children to explore the ocean and experiment with this interactive activity.

MATERIALS

- Template (page 72)
- White (or other color) paint
- Medium blue backing cardstock
- Construction paper in various colors, including yellow and light blue
- 3 cardstock strips in any color
- Cardboard/paper tube
- Green tissue paper
- Scissors
- Glue stick
- Pencil
- Paintbrush

Paper Folding Technique:
Loop

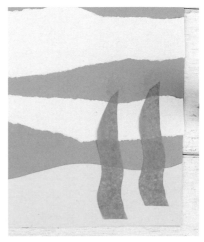

1. Start the background. We need an under-the-sea habitat! Cut a wave into the long edge of a sheet of yellow paper and glue this wavy yellow strip along the bottom of a sheet of medium blue backing cardstock.

2. Add more blue water. Take a sheet of light blue paper and tear it into strips. Glue the torn strips to the under-the-sea background—the light blue against the medium blue will create a lovely contrast.

3. Make the seaweed. Cut out a few wavy strips from pieces of green tissue paper to resemble seaweed. Glue this seaweed to the sandy area to complete the under-the-sea habitat.

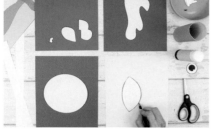

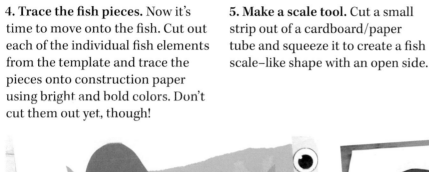

4. Trace the fish pieces. Now it's time to move onto the fish. Cut out each of the individual fish elements from the template and trace the pieces onto construction paper using bright and bold colors. Don't cut them out yet, though!

5. Make a scale tool. Cut a small strip out of a cardboard/paper tube and squeeze it to create a fish scale–like shape with an open side.

6. Add scales and cut out. Dip the scale tool into white paint and use it to make scaly prints across the body (the large circle) of the fish. Fill the body circle with prints. After the paint dries, cut out all the traced fish elements.

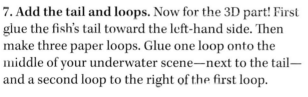

7. Add the tail and loops. Now for the 3D part! First glue the fish's tail toward the left-hand side. Then make three paper loops. Glue one loop onto the middle of your underwater scene—next to the tail—and a second loop to the right of the first loop.

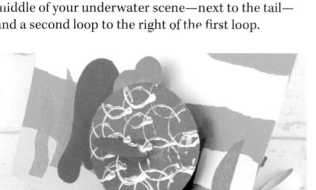

8. Attach the body. Add fins to the body of the fish. Glue the top fin to the top of the fish's body. Create a small fold in the side fin and apply glue to this area, then glue it to the body so the fin sticks out. Glue the fish's body onto the two cardstock loops. Make sure you don't cover the back of the body with glue, otherwise the fish might end up stuck to the background!

9. Attach the head. Let's give our fish some extra bounce! Glue the third cardstock loop onto the right-hand side of the fish's body. Assemble the fish's head with the eye and mouth. Then, just like you did with the body, carefully glue the fish's head onto the loop. Now the tropical fish can explore the colorful ocean habitat!

Giraffe

If you're looking for a healthy dose of fun in the savanna, then look no further than this sunny paper craft. Children can discover why the giraffe's neck is so long as they help their bobbing, bouncing friend reach up for the tall leaves. Will your kids carefully craft a realistic giraffe, or will they let their imaginations run wild to create their very own colorful rainbow scene?

MATERIALS

- Template (pages 70 and 71)
- Favorite coloring medium (such as paint, crayons, or paint sticks)
- Blue backing cardstock
- 2 orange cardstock strips
- Green tissue paper
- Black marker
- Scissors
- Glue stick

Paper Folding Technique: Loop

1. Add spots. What makes a giraffe unique? His spots! So, on the template, draw some large spots on his neck and some smaller ones around his face (the large oval). Remember, a giraffe's spots aren't a uniform shape—they're like wobbly circles and squares! Then paint or color in the giraffe. You can create a realistic giraffe with brown, orange, and yellow, or go for a colorful rainbow one—it's up to you!

2. Add leaves. Now we need to give our giraffe some leaves to nibble on. Carefully cut some leaf shapes out of green tissue paper. It's even better if you have two different shades of green, as it will give your trees some depth. Glue the leaves, layering up the colors, around the edges of the blue cardstock. Don't forget to leave space in the middle for your giraffe!

3. Start the giraffe assembly. First, glue the horns and eyes onto the face and set the face aside. Then glue the giraffe's neck onto the leafy blue background, making sure you place it at the bottom of the page, roughly in the middle.

4. Add paper loops. Create two loops from one strip of orange cardstock cut in half. Glue one of the loops just above the giraffe's neck, then glue the second loop an inch or two (a few centimeters) above the first loop. This is how you'll make your giraffe's head pop up.

5. Add the head. Carefully glue the giraffe's head onto the two cardstock loops. Make sure you don't cover the back of the head with glue, otherwise your giraffe might end up totally stuck to the background! Then take another strip of orange cardstock and create a large third loop. Glue this one onto the middle of the giraffe's face.

6. Add the nose. On the mouth, draw a smile just below the giraffe's nostrils, then, just like you did with his face, carefully glue his nose onto the last loop.

Hedgehog

Be inspired by nature's changing colors and textures with this super simple but really effective 3D craft. Incorporating an autumn scavenger hunt, this is a fun and interactive way for children to get outside into nature and discover how they can transform what they've found into art. They'll be amazed at how a handful of twigs, seeds, and leaves can create a gorgeous hedgehog that looks like she snuffled right out of a hedgerow!

MATERIALS

- Template (page 73)
- Green backing cardstock
- Pink and dark red cardstock or construction paper
- Autumn shades of paper—red, yellow, and orange
- Dry natural materials, such as acorns, shells, and mini pine cones
- Black pom-pom
- Black marker
- Glue stick
- White/PVA glue (optional)
- Pencil

1. Trace all the shapes. Cut out the individual hedgehog elements from the template. Trace the lower body onto pink paper, the oval onto dark red paper, and the leaf shape multiple times onto the autumn paper shades (red, yellow, and orange).

2. Cut out the shapes. Cut out all the traced elements. For an extra-fine motor workout, when cutting out the dark red oval, place the template on top of it and use the zigzag dotted lines on the template as a guide to cut spikes.

Small shells, acorns, and other natural materials are a choking hazard for young children; ensure adequate adult supervision.

3. Make the body. Assemble the body on a piece of green backing cardstock, adding the eye and a cute black pom-pom nose.

5. Add leaves. Once you've added some of the natural elements, fill in some of the gaps with your paper leaves. Fold each leaf in half lengthwise, then glue just one half to the body, allowing the other to stick out.

6. Finish the body. Continue building up the hedgehog by adding smaller filler natural items until the body is full of texture and paper leaves.

4. Decorate with natural items. Apply a generous amount of glue to the spiky oval and begin adding your natural items. Start with larger items and work your way to smaller ones. Items without a flat edge, such as acorns and pine cones, may need a stronger adhesive like white/PVA glue rather than a glue stick.

7. Add a smile. Complete the hedgehog by using a black marker to draw on a cute expression—how about a smile?

Insects

We think crafts should be for everyone—you shouldn't have to spend a fortune at the store to have fun and make something special! All kids need for these cute insects is a few cardboard tubes, some imagination, and plenty of creativity! They're perfect for a quick and eco-friendly craft session.

MATERIALS

- Template (pages 74 and 75)
- Favorite coloring medium (such as paint, crayons, or paint sticks)
- Black paint (optional)
- Black, yellow, and light purple or blue construction paper
- Cardboard/paper tubes
- Black yarn or string
- Black marker
- Scissors
- Paintbrush (optional)

1. Color the template. Color in the ladybug, bee, and butterfly templates and carefully cut out each of the elements.

2. Start wrapping a tube. Cut a strip of yellow paper that is slightly wider than the tube. Apply glue to one end of the strip, secure it to the tube, and start to roll.

3. Finish the wrap. After you've completely covered the tube with paper, secure the other end with a second application of glue. Fold the excess paper around the ends to the inside of the tube. Wrap a second tube with light purple/blue and a third tube with black (or paint the black tube as we have done).

4. Cut the ladybug's wings. The black tube is for the ladybug. We want her to fly, so cut the spotted heart shape in half vertically to create her wings.

5. Finish the ladybug. Glue the wings onto the black tube, angled with the pointed ends together and round ends apart. Then complete the ladybug by gluing on her eyes and antennae.

6. Make the bee's stripes. Make two small cuts into the yellow tube, one at each end. Slot one end of the black yarn into one cut. Then wrap the yarn down around the tube to make lovely fuzzy stripes. Secure the other end into the second slot you cut.

7. Finish the bee. Glue on the bee's wings, eyes, and antennae—and why not draw on a big friendly smile, too?

8. Add the butterfly's face. Glue the butterfly's eyes and antennae to purple/blue tube. Use a black marker to draw a lovely smile.

9. Add the butterfly's wings. Separate the cut-out butterfly wings into two pairs, each with a large and small wing. Glue the smaller wing along the bottom of the larger wing as shown for both pairs. Then apply a generous amount of glue along the flat edge of each set of wings and secure them to the back of the tube.

Jellyfish

Are your children learning all about ocean animals? Or perhaps they're just dreaming of the beach! Either way, they'll love this colorful summer-themed craft where the jellyfish wibble, wobble, and pop from the page! The variety of techniques included, from coloring and cutting to tearing and gluing, makes it a great activity for exercising those all-important fine motor skills.

MATERIALS

- Template (page 76)
- Watercolor paint
- Dark blue backing cardstock
- Light blue and yellow cardstock or construction paper
- 4 light blue cardstock strips
- Colorful yarn
- Scissors
- Glue stick
- Paintbrush

Paper Folding Technique: Accordion

1. Paint the template. Paint the jellyfish template with watercolor paint. Watercolors usually dry quickly and can produce vibrant colors, making them a fantastic medium to explore with kids! If you don't have any watercolors, you can use regular paint or crayons.

2. Make the water. Tear a sheet of light blue cardstock into strips. Align the straight edges and glue a few strips to the dark blue cardstock. The contrasting blues will create an effective under-the-sea backdrop for the swimming jellyfish.

3. Add the sand. Complete the background with some wavy sand by cutting a wavy line across some yellow cardstock and gluing it to the bottom of the background.

4. Prep the jellyfish and seaweed. Cut out all the template elements. Glue the eyes to the jellyfish bodies, then add the seaweed to the underwater backdrop.

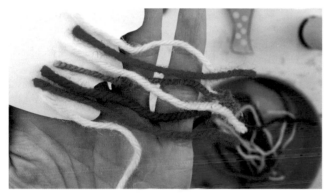

5. Add the tentacles. Cut a bunch of strips of yarn. Apply a layer of glue along the wavy jellyfish bottoms, then add a row of the strips of yarn to each jellyfish.

6. Make two accordions. Make two accordions from the blue cardstock strips and glue one end of each to the underwater backdrop where you want to place your two jellyfish.

7. Attach the jellyfish. Add dabs of glue to the tops of each accordion and place a jellyfish on top, pushing them down to ensure they're secure. Now the jellyfish will jiggle and wiggle as they swim in their beautiful underwater habitat!

Kite

Let's go fly a kite, with this bright and colorful paper craft! This tactile rainbow-colored activity is the ultimate way to explore depth and perspective as both the kite and string pop from the page. Utilizing buttons and ribbon as well as paper, children will be amazed that they can create such impressive art simply with paper folding.

MATERIALS

- Template (page 77)
- Blue backing cardstock
- 7 (or more) pieces of cardstock in at least 6 different rainbow colors
- Ribbon
- Buttons
- Pipe cleaner
- Scissors
- Glue stick
- Pencil

Paper Folding Technique: Zigzag

1. Prep the template pieces. Cut out the template elements and glue the clouds to the blue backing cardstock. This will become the backdrop for the flying kite.

2. Cut the kite pieces. Trace the kite shape onto at least seven sheets of colored cardstock (one can be a duplicate color) and cut all the pieces out. This example demonstrates a rainbow kite—but your kite could be all one color or patterned with two or more colors.

3. Attach the kite base. Glue one kite shape (the duplicate color, if you have one) to the backing cardstock.

> Buttons are a choking hazard for young children; ensure adequate adult supervision.

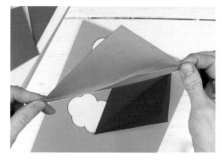

4. Fold the kite pieces. Fold each of the remaining kite shapes in half. Next, apply glue to one half of one folded kite shape and secure the sticky side to one half of the kite base on the background.

5. Start layering the kite pieces. Apply glue to the side that is sticking up on the kite shape that you just attached. Then layer a second folded kite shape on top of that, the same way you attached the first one to the background.

6. Add the rest of the kite pieces. Continuing layering the folded kites on one side, positioning one on top of the other and aligning the shapes as you go along.

7. Finish the kite. Once you've used up all the folded kites, apply a generous amount of glue to the remaining part of the kite base on the backing cardstock, then press down the layered kites to the glue. The kite has now popped!

8. Make two bows. Using leftover cardstock from when you cut out the kite shapes, cut out two wide rectangles. Fold each one into a long zigzag (folding from the short side). Wrap a small piece of pipe cleaner around the center of each folded piece and open the folds to create a bow.

9. Add the decorations. Glue a piece of ribbon to the kite for a tail, adding a twirly, whirly effect by gluing some sections with extra ribbon pushed up to give the tail lift. Glue the paper bows to the ribbon, and hide the pipe cleaner wraps by decorating each one with a large button.

Lion

This impressive craft focuses on the lion's pride and glory: his mane. Ideal for slightly older children, this craft uses layers of carefully curled paper to create the texture of thick fur. Children can explore color and create extra depth by using different shades of yellow and orange paper, and they can even use wrapping paper scraps for a touch of extra creative embellishment!

MATERIALS

- Template (page 82)
- Orange and yellow paint
- Lots of yellow and orange shades of construction paper strips in various colors, patterns, widths, and lengths
- Paper plate

- String
- Black marker
- Scissors
- Glue stick
- Paintbrush

Paper Folding Technique: Curl

1. Paint the paper plate. Using a mixture of orange and yellow shades, paint the paper plate and allow to dry.

2. Start making coils. Gather at least forty construction paper strips. Wrap each strip of paper around the tip of a paintbrush or pencil to create a tight coil. Then slide the paper off the rolling form and allow the coil to naturally unravel.

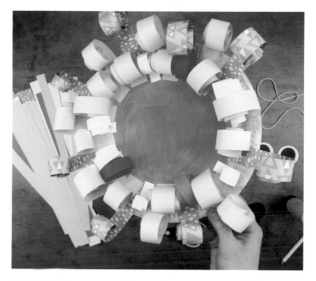

3. Start creating the mane. Starting from around the outside of the paper plate, begin gluing on the curled strips of paper. Make sure you apply a generous amount of glue to each strand and press down on the sticky area for a few seconds before moving on to the next curl.

4. Finish the mane. Once the outer rim of the paper plate is full with curls, work on adding an inner ring of curls. Some curls will be tighter than others—the variation of curls and colors will only add to the texture of the lion's mane!

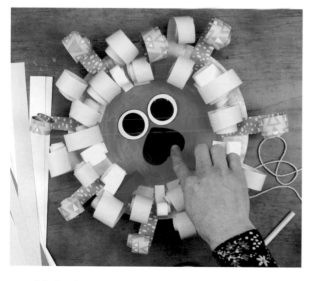

5. Add the face. Cut out the eyes and nose from the template. Glue them to the center of the paper plate. Add a little smile with a black marker.

6. Add the whiskers. Complete the lion by adding a set of whiskers made from short lengths of string.

Melting Snowman

This wintery craft flips the way children think about perspective, because, instead of jumping out from the page, it represents a snowman shrinking down. It's a really fun and engaging way to think about the idea of melting snow—but kids needn't be sad, because their friendly snowman can always pop back up again!

MATERIALS

- Template (page 78)
- Blue chalk or crayon
- Blue backing cardstock
- 4 white cardstock strips
- Cotton balls/wool/stuffing
- Scissors
- Glue stick

Paper Folding Technique: Accordion

1. Add the melting effect. Using a piece of blue chalk, draw random blue lines all around the two blob-like shapes on the template. Rub the lines with your finger and drag inward to create depth. This subtle touch adds to the impression of snow melting into water. You can also use a crayon to create a similar effect.

2. Prep the pieces. Carefully cut out the melting snowman elements. Also create two accordions using the white cardstock strips.

3. Attach the base. Cut a sheet of blue cardstock in half or slightly larger. Glue the largest snowman piece to center of the large piece. Then glue one accordion to the center.

4. Add buttons. Next, glue two of the "lost" buttons and an arm on top of the snowman piece and backing cardstock in a semi-random placement.

5. Add the middle. Glue the medium-sized white snowman piece to the top of the accordion. Add the second accordion to the center of this middle piece, then glue on the remaining arm and the last button so they stick out at the edges.

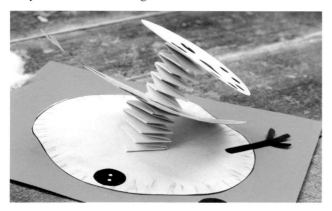

6. Add the head. Complete the three-part snowman by gluing the head to the top of the second accordion. The snowman will now both pop out and melt down with a push of a finger!

7. Add snow. Add a little glue to the edges and corners of the blue backing cardstock, then rip up some cotton (you may also use wool or stuffing) to stick all around the edges. This frames the "puddle of water" created by the melting snowman.

Nest with Chick

We love an alternative Easter craft, so if you're tired of eggs, have a go at this cute nest instead. Kids will love making the sweet little chick, with her flappy wings and googly eyes, and then creating a safe and snuggly nest for her. They can use straw or tear strips of paper, or they could even go outside and collect some twigs and leaves—while they're out there, see if they can they spot any real nests in the trees!

MATERIALS

- Template (page 79)
- Brown, yellow, blue, and orange paint
- Paper plate
- Craft stick/Popsicle® stick
- Googly eyes
- Craft straw
- Black marker
- Hole punch (optional)
- Scissors
- Glue stick
- White/PVA glue
- Paintbrush

1. Paint the pieces. Paint the chick template and paper plate, making the plate half blue and half brown. Allow both to thoroughly dry.

2. Create a slit. Carefully bend the plate in half (without creating a crease) and cut a slit into the brown area of the plate, not far off from the center.

3. Check the fit. Open up the plate and place the craft stick up through the slit from the back side. Check that the craft stick can easily move from side to side, then remove it. If necessary, refold the plate and make the cut a little longer.

4. Start making the chick. Using a black marker, add feathery doodle details to the chick's body. Next, cut out all the elements and begin assembling the puppet onto the craft stick, starting with the body and wings.

5. Finish the chick. Add facial elements to the chick's head—the beak, some googly eyes, and some optional cheeks (made from hole-punched pink paper). Glue the head to the top of the body. The puppet is complete!

7. Get playing! Allow the glue on the paper plate and straw to completely dry. Then insert the chick puppet down through the slit and play!

6. Make the nest. Apply a generous amount of white/PVA glue directly to the brown area of the paper plate. Fill the area with craft straw, allowing the strands to pop from the paper plate. Some strands can remain long, others can be cut short. Avoid covering the slit you created earlier.

Owls

Take cardboard tube crafts to the next level with this bright and fun owl activity! Once children have created the basic owl shape, they can really use their creativity and let their personalities shine through with the decorations. Circles of tissue paper are a great way to play with color, depth, and texture, as kids can layer them up and discover what effects they can create.

MATERIALS

- Template (page 82)
- Paint sticks or crayons
- White and various other colors of paint
- Various colors of paper, including orange or yellow
- Cardboard/paper tubes
- Scissors
- Glue stick
- Pencil
- Paintbrush

1. Paint the tubes. If you're using pre-purchased cardboard tubes made for crafting, the size is already fine. If you're using paper towel tubes, cut the tubes in half. Paint each of the three tubes first with a coat of white and then with a color of your choice. This two-layered approach will enhance the top color, leaving a bright and beautiful finish.

2. Push the sides in. Once the tubes have dried, it's time to create the owl ear shapes. Starting at the top of each tube, gently push the middle area inward on one side. Repeat on the other side of the top of the tube to create two distinctive pointed tips. Make these pointed tips on all three tubes.

3. Cut the owl pieces. Carefully cut out all the template elements. Trace the wings onto brightly colored paper and the beak onto orange or yellow paper. Trace the feather shape six times per owl onto an existing piece of artwork, or you can quickly create something new with crayons or paint sticks. Cut out all the traced elements.

4. Add the feathers. Glue the feathers in an overlapping three-two-one formation, starting from the bottom of the tube with a row of three, then adding a row of two, then adding a single feather.

5. Add the beak. Fold the beak in half and glue it to the tube just above the top feather, overlapping it slightly.

6. Add the eyes. Select a pair of eyes. Will your owl be on high alert with big, open eyes, or a little sleepy? Glue the eyes on either side of the beak, overlapping it slightly.

7. Add the wings. Complete your owl by gluing the wings to either side of the body. Make more owl friends so that they can flock together!

Polar Bear

Whether you're looking for a winter-themed craft or one to support an Arctic school project, this cheerful, friendly polar bear is guaranteed to bring a smile to children's faces. And it's a great way to demonstrate that there are different ways to create depth! Kids will love building the bear's body up and watching him grow—then making him pop even more with a colorful, contrasting textured background.

MATERIALS

- Template (pages 80 and 81)
- Blue backing cardstock
- Pink, lilac, and light blue paper
- 3 white cardstock strips
- Scissors
- Glue stick

Paper Folding Techniques:
Loop
Accordion

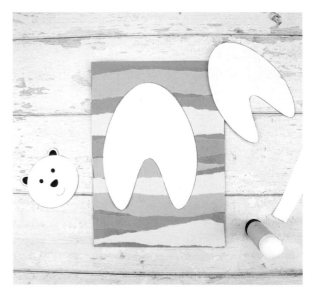

1. Make the background. Rip a bunch of strips of pink, lilac, and light blue paper. Layer the strips from top to bottom on the blue backing cardstock, leaving some gaps to reveal the color beneath. This will create a beautiful blend of colors that will enhance the pop of the white polar bear.

2. Start assembling the polar bear. Cut out the polar bear template elements. Glue the ears to the bear's head and glue the large body piece to the Arctic background.

3. Add lifting loops. Make two white paper loops using a single cardstock strip cut in half. Secure one to the center of the polar bear and the other one lower and slightly offset from the foot area.

4. Add the middle of the bear. Add a dab of glue to the top of both loops and place the smaller body piece of the bear on top.

5. Add an accordion. Make an accordion from two strips of white cardstock. Glue one end of the accordion to the center of the polar bear's second level.

6. Finish the bear. Glue the polar bear's head on top of the accordion. With the polar bear now complete, the body will bounce while the head will stretch and wobble!

Queen

This royal craft is sure to please even the most discerning queen. Children can have fun using paper to create different 3D elements, from the queen's curled hair to her proud bejeweled crown. Why not encourage them to make crowns for themselves, too?

MATERIALS

- Template (pages 84 and 85)
- Watercolor paint
- Any color backing cardstock
- Lots of strips of colored construction paper
- Scissors
- Glue stick
- Paintbrush

Paper Folding Technique: Curl

1. Color the pieces. Using watercolors, color in the queen's head, adding a skin tone, blushing cheeks, and perhaps distinctive facial features such as freckles or moles. Why not grab a mirror and paint the queen in your own image? Don't forget to color in the crown and jewels.

2. Cut out the pieces. Carefully cut out the template elements. Glue the jewels onto the crown in a pattern you like.

3. Add the head and hair. Center the queen's head at the bottom of a piece of backing cardstock and glue it down. Then start framing the queen's face with glued-down strips of paper.

4. Curl the hair. You can leave the hair strips straight, or you can curl them. To curl, simply roll the paper around the tip of a paintbrush or pencil, then gently remove the rolled paper from the rolling form and allow it to naturally unfold to reveal the curl.

5. Add bangs. Continue framing the queen's head with curled or straight paper until her head is full. You can layer strips, cut them to different lengths, or fold or curl tightly to create different effects.

6. Add the crown. Gently bend the crown in half without creasing it, bringing the two ends to meet. Apply a thick layer of glue to the colored side of each end of the crown. Then stick the crown to the backing cardstock, just above the queen's hairline, by bending these glued areas around to the back.

Reindeer

Not overtly festive, this reindeer craft would be equally as perfect for a general winter or Arctic animal activity as it would be for Christmas. As well as his cheerful nose, this reindeer has an extra-special 3D element: personalized antlers made with your children's handprints. This is a fun and engaging craft that kids will love making and that you'll want to keep out on display.

MATERIALS

- Template (page 83)
- Blue backing cardstock
- Brown, yellow, red, and white paper
- 4 yellow cardstock strips
- Large hole punch or circular items to trace, such as jar lids and coins
- Scissors
- Glue stick
- Pencil

Paper Folding Technique: Accordion

1. Create snow. Create a snowy backdrop by gluing white paper circles to a sheet of blue cardstock. Make the circles with a large hole punch or simply trace around circular objects, such as jar lids or coins.

2. Cut the first set of pieces. This reindeer is made up of circles and ovals. The shapes within the template need to be cut in three phases, not all at once. To start, trace the largest oval (the one that is a set of three) and the small ear ovals onto brown paper and cut out.

3. Cut the second set of pieces. Cut out the second-largest oval (of the set of three). Then trace this onto brown paper and cut out. Next, cut out the circle (of the set of three). Then trace this circle onto red paper. Finally, cut out the small ovals within the ears, then trace these shapes onto yellow paper.

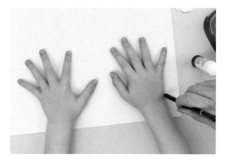

4. Cut the antlers. Finally, trace around a pair of hands, then cut out the two hand shapes. These will be the antlers!

5. Start assembling the reindeer. Glue each small yellow oval to a brown counterpart to become ears. Glue the ears to the top of the second largest oval just where it begins to narrow. Glue the red nose to the center of the large oval.

6. Attach the head and eyes. Glue the head a few inches (a few centimeters) down from the top of the snowy backdrop, leaving enough room for the antlers above it. Add a pair of eyes to the reindeer's head.

7. Fold the nose. Gently fold the narrow ends of the large nose oval inward to create two flaps. Apply lots of glue to each flap. Then gently bend the entire oval to make it into an arch shape, without creating a crease.

8. Attach the nose. Glue one folded flap of the nose to the snowy backdrop, just below the bottom of the reindeer's face. Keeping the arch shape, glue the other flap to the other side of the reindeer's face. You now have some lovely depth and perspective.

9. Add the antlers. Make two accordions using the yellow cardstock strips. Glue them both above the reindeer's head. Then glue a handprint to the top of each accordion.

Spider

Incorporating coloring, careful cutting, gluing, and folding, this is a perfect activity to reinforce fine motor skills, and as it brings movement and dimension to paper crafting, it's also really engaging for kids of all ages. Most importantly, though, it's fun to play with!

MATERIALS

- Template (pages 86 and 87)
- Favorite coloring medium (such as paint, crayons, or paint sticks)
- Black cardstock
- String
- Paper straw
- Scissors
- Glue stick
- Pencil

Paper Folding Technique: Zigzag

1. Color in the template. Paint or color in the spiderweb. Go for bold, bright colors; you could even create patterns and doodles on top for an extra vibrant pop!

2. Cut out the pieces. Carefully cut out all the spider elements from the template (except for the web, which stays a full page). Use the rectangle templates as a guide to cut two black cardstock rectangles. Use the dotted line rectangle template to cut eight even legs into one black rectangle. This is great cutting practice—try and keep a straight, steady hand!

3. Fold the legs. Fold each spider leg using a zigzag fold. Then give some of them a twist in order to create wild, wriggly legs.

4. Prepare the body. Take the second black rectangle and bend it around to make a big loop. Secure the end with a lot of glue so it doesn't come undone.

5. Assemble the body. Glue the legs onto the back of the loop, then glue on the eyes and mouth.

6. Cut slits. Gently bend one end of the web sheet and carefully cut two slits as shown, using the tips of the web on the template as a guide, so that your spider has a place to dangle from.

7. Add the straw. Thread a paper straw through the two slits you just made so that the ends of the straw are on the back of the sheet.

8. Tie on the spider. Cut a long piece of string or yarn (about the same length as the spiderweb), then wrap it through the loop of the spider's body, around the back of the loop. Tie it into a knot. Tie the other end of the string securely around the paper straw on the front of the spiderweb sheet.

9. Ready to play! Ta-dah—the spider is ready to bounce, wobble, and play on his colorful web. He's so cute that surely no one could be scared of him!

Tree

We love to incorporate different mediums and textures into our crafts, especially bits and pieces we often have lying around the house. This gorgeous, expressive tree craft uses sticks for the trunk contrasted with curled paper branches and button leaves. It creates a really interesting juxtaposition between natural and man-made materials. Children can choose buttons in a color theme, like red, orange, and yellow, to make a tree perfect for fall, or embrace all the colors of the rainbow.

MATERIALS

- White backing cardstock
- 2 shades of green paper
- At least 7 brown paper strips, cut thin
- Sticks/twigs

- Buttons in many colors
- Scissors
- Glue stick
- White/PVA glue
- Paintbrush or pencil

Paper Folding Technique:
Curl

1. Cut grass pieces. Cut two rectangles of green paper the full width of the paper sheet, making the darker green rectangle larger than the lighter green one. Then cut random triangular shapes into one long edge of each rectangle. These pieces will become part of a grassy floor for the tree. Including two shades will add a sense of perspective to the craft.

2. Add one grass piece and prep your strips. Glue the dark grassy strip to the white cardstock, aligning the bottom to the bottom of the cardstock. Set the light grassy strip aside for later. Then make sure your brown strips are cut thinly, thinner than you would normally use for making loops or accordions.

3. Make a branch. Roll one brown paper strip around a pencil or paintbrush like you would to create a curl, but wrap it up the entire length of the item rather than over and over again around the same spot.

> Buttons are a choking hazard for young children; ensure adequate adult supervision.

4. Attach one branch. Glue one end of the paper strip to the center upper area of the cardstock. Pull the paper strip away from the center to open up the curl and apply glue to the points where the curl meets the backing cardstock.

5. Add more branches. Repeat this process to fill the surrounding white space with the rest of the branches for the tree.

6. Add the trunk. Secure the sticks/twigs with white/PVA glue. Whatever the shape or length of your twigs, make sure they start from the bottom of the backing cardstock and meet the curly paper branches, covering the glued-down branch ends.

7. Add more grass. Add the lighter green grassy strip over the trunk of the tree. This will provide extra support to the twigs and add to the overall 3D effect. You can even add some individual grassy spikes in the darker green color on top.

8. Add background buttons. Fill the space between the branches with colorful buttons, gluing them on with more white/PVA glue. We created a rainbow tree—your kids may enjoy this twist, or they may use the concept to create a seasonally relevant tree: pink and white buttons for spring, or red, yellow, orange, and brown for fall, etc.!

9. Finish adding buttons. Glue more buttons under the branches and even on top of some of the curls. Be careful when gluing to the tops of the curls to allow each button to dry before touching that curl again, or you might knock off the still-wet buttons.

Unicorn

Is there a child around who doesn't love a unicorn? With this mythical activity, kids can explore contrast with light and shade, depth and perspective with a mix of 2D and 3D elements, and different mediums as they play with paint, cardstock, and yarn. Unleash the magic with this expressive and impactful unicorn art.

MATERIALS

- Template (page 90)
- Blue, purple, red, white, and yellow paint
- Colored backing cardstock
- Black cardstock
- Scrap paper
- At least 12 paper strips in various colors, cut thin
- Yarn in various colors

- Craft stick/Popsicle® stick
- Hole punch
- Sponge
- Scissors
- Glue stick
- Paintbrush
- Clear adhesive tape

Paper Folding Technique: Curl

 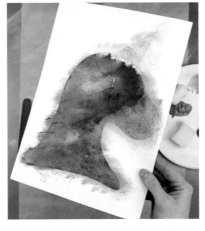 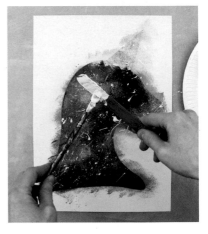

1. Start coloring the template. Cut the template out, trace it on black cardstock, cut the black piece out, and temporarily tape the piece to a sheet of scrap paper. Apply a dark paint color, such as blue, to a piece of sponge. Gently dab in a random fashion across the unicorn. Don't dab the horn.

2. Finish coloring. Using a clean sponge, blend white into areas of the first color and move across the template, dabbing different areas of the unicorn. Continue the process of adding both light and dark colors, blending as you go, to create a gorgeous galaxy effect. Focus on just light colors, like yellow and white, for the horn.

3. Add white speckles. Apply a generous amount of white paint to a bristly paintbrush. Use a craft stick (or another spare tool that you can clean later) to brush against the paintbrush and create controlled splats across the unicorn. The splats will produce a real galaxy effect on the unicorn.

4. Punch mane holes. Once the unicorn has dried, remove it from the scrap paper. Punch evenly spaced holes along the back of the head and neck.

5. Cut strands for the first knot. Gather a bright selection of yarn. Select two or three colors and cut a bunch of strands, each approximately the same length as the backing cardstock.

6. Thread the strands through. Thread the bunch of strands through one of the holes along the neck so that you have an equal length on either side of the hole. Create a knot to secure the set of strands to the hole (see next step).

7. Continue knotting. To make a knot, first gather the yarn strands all together so that you have a loop at one end and the strand ends at the other; then thread the collected strands back through the yarn loop. Shown here is the second set of strands before tightening the knot. Continue cutting sets of strands and knotting them through each hole.

8. Attach the unicorn. Apply glue all over the back of the unicorn almost up to the yarn/holes, leaving the remaining space up to the edge of the shape along the mane clear of glue. Secure the unicorn to a sheet of backing cardstock.

9. Add paper curls. Make paper curls by wrapping a selection of two or three paper strands at a time around a paintbrush or pencil. Remove them and glue the flat area of the paper under the unicorn's head, positioning the curls between the knotted strands of yarn. Continue until the whole mane is lined with paper curls between the yarn.

Vase with Flower

Ideal for Mother's Day, Easter, or spring/summer colors, kids will love getting hands-on with this floral craft. Both the vase and flower are 3D, but they are created using different techniques, so it's the perfect craft to really help children express themselves. They can snip, curl, color, and scrunch their way to a beautiful greeting card or piece of art for display.

MATERIALS

- Template (page 94)
- Favorite coloring medium (such as paint, crayons, or paint sticks)
- White backing cardstock
- At least 6 paper strips each in at least 2 different colors

- Green, orange, and yellow tissue paper
- Scissors
- Glue stick
- Clear adhesive tape (optional)

Paper Folding Technique:
Loop (with flattened end)

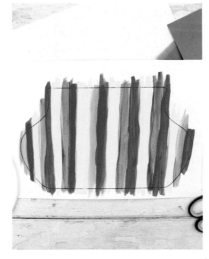

1. Color the template. Decorate the template with your desired coloring medium. Create a pattern like the stripes shown here, or draw a unique design.

2. Cut the slits. Cut out the vase and fold it in half horizontally, without creasing it, starting the fold a little after the curve. Carefully cut about five slits along the fold, all centered below the neck of the vase.

3. Glue the ends. Unfold the vase, then gently bend the vase around until the curvy flaps on either side overlap. Secure these flaps together with glue or tape.

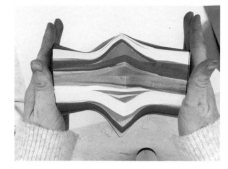

4. Finish the vase. Place the vase between your hands and push together gently until the middle area pops where all the slits were cut. Then use a generous amount of glue to affix the vase so that the bottom aligns with the bottom of the backing cardstock.

5. Make the stem. Take a piece of green tissue paper and twist it to create a thin, long stem. Glue the stem inside the vase so that part of it sticks out above the top of the vase.

6. Make the first petal loop. Starting with a darker color paper strip, bend the strip in half (without creasing it) and secure the ends together with glue. This makes a loop with a flattened end. Glue this loop to the tip of the stem.

7. Add more petals. Add six or more petals (depending on the width of your strips) in a circular formation to complete the outer flower petals.

8. Add an inner ring of petals. Trim a new set of paper strips in a different, lighter color to be somewhat shorter than the previous set of petal strips. Glue these down inside the first ring of petals, filling in the gaps.

9. Add the flower center. Fill the center of the flower with scrunched-up balls of tissue paper, gluing down orange first and then yellow on top of that.

Winter Blooms

Explore the changing seasons with this lovely and unusual 3D flower craft. Using crinkly tissue paper, bendy and fuzzy pipe cleaners, and soft, fluffy cotton, it's a really tactile and sensory activity. But it's also great for those fine motor skills, as children have to work carefully, petal by petal, to build their crocuses and bring their snowy garden to life.

MATERIALS

- Paper plate
- Tissue paper in various colors, including green and yellow
- Green pipe cleaners
- Cotton balls/wool/stuffing
- Scissors
- White/PVA glue
- Clear adhesive tape (or colored tape, if you have some)

1. Make stem holes. Using scissors, pierce three or more holes into the center of the paper plate and thread a green pipe cleaner through each hole. Each pipe cleaner will become a single flower—a crocus, the first kind of flower to bloom when spring is on the way.

2. Trim and secure the stems. Secure the pipe cleaners onto the top side of the plate by twirling each end flat against the plate and securing it in place with a piece of tape. Turn the paper plate over and cut the pipe cleaners down to stems of a couple inches (about 5 centimeters) each. Don't throw away the trimmed ends—we'll use them later.

3. Cut the flower centers. For each pipe cleaner stem, cut a rectangle shape from two pieces of layered yellow tissue paper. So, for three crocuses, you'll need six rectangles.

4. Add a flower center. Wrap a set of two yellow rectangles around the tip of a pipe cleaner. Then tightly wrap a cutoff end of a pipe cleaner around the tissue paper to secure it to the stem.

5. Snip the flower center. Cut some shallow incisions into the top of the yellow tissue paper, then spread the pieces out. The yellow tissue paper has become the middle, or stamen, of the crocus. Add a stamen to your other flowers now.

6. Cut the petals. Cut out four to six petal shapes each from brightly colored pieces of tissue paper, choosing a different color for each crocus. Add glue to the bottom of just one petal and wrap it around a stamen, securing it to the pipe cleaner.

7. Glue all the petals. Add a second tissue paper petal opposite the first, and then a third and fourth petal between the first pair. Add more petals if you want to. Then create the other flowers the same way.

8. Add leaves. Cut thin, pointy strips of green tissue paper and glue a couple to the base of each stem, sticking up.

9. Add snow. Complete the winter garden by filling the bottom of the paper plate with cotton balls (you may also use wool or stuffing) to create the impression of a snowy landscape. Make sure you use lots of gooey white/PVA glue to secure the "snow" in place.

Xylophone

Combining craft, play, and learning, this is such a fun item to make, particularly for younger kids. Children can explore color, order, and size, choosing which way to build their xylophone—and then have lots of fun "playing" it!

MATERIALS

- Template (pages 88 and 89)
- Favorite coloring medium (such as paint, crayons, or paint sticks)
- Scissors
- Glue stick

1. Color in the template. Color in the xylophone template with a medium of your choice. We suggest making the keys in rainbow colors.

2. Cut out the pieces. Carefully cut out the xylophone mallets and rectangular keys, including cutting all the keys into individual strips. Leave the large base piece uncut.

3. Attach the first key. Gently fold the ends of the first paper strip and apply glue to the folded areas. Using the "X" of the xylophone base as a guide and starting from the widest part of the base, glue down one fold. Gently bend the strip across to the opposite side and glue the other fold down to create the first rainbow arch.

4. Continue attaching keys. Now that we have the first arch, the kids will need to engage their problem-solving skills to work out how the remaining "keys" should fit along the xylophone.

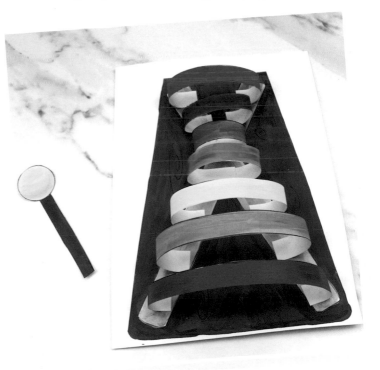

5. Shorten strips as desired. As kids progress along the xylophone, some strips of paper will need to be shortened—or the arches could simply be made bigger. The choice is theirs! This is a great opportunity for the kids to consider pattern formation and sequencing.

6. Finish the keys. Continue filling the xylophone with rainbow arches. The instrument is done and ready to play!

Yarn-Wrapped Bird

Encourage children to explore their creativity and versatility, as well as consider the environment, with this tactile craft combining natural and recycled or scrap materials. Kids can play with color and texture and hone their fine motor skills with considered cuts and careful yarn threading to create a beautiful springtime bird.

MATERIALS

- Template (page 91)
- Scrap cardboard
- Scrap colored paper, tissue paper, or packaging paper
- Yarn
- Scrap lace, ribbon, stickers, or eco-friendly glitter
- Wooden clothespins
- Stick (optional)
- Scissors
- White/PVA glue
- Pencil

1. Cut out the pieces. Cut out the elements from the template. Trace and cut out the beak from yellow paper. Trace the body and the wing onto a piece of scrap cardboard, then cut out these two cardboard pieces. It will be a little trickier to cut cardboard than to cut paper or cardstock, so cut slowly and carefully.

2. Prepare the body. Cut little slits all around the edge of the bird's body, each about half an inch (a centimeter) apart. Scrunch up a piece of scrap paper into a ball and glue it to the head area of the cardboard body. This will give the bird extra depth and emphasis to the head.

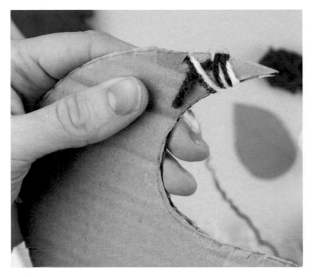

3. Start wrapping with yarn. Starting at the tail, build the bird's colorful feathers by wrapping two strings of yarn around the bird at a time, slotting them into the slits as you go to keep it in place.

4. Finish wrapping. Continue wrapping all the way around the body, ensuring the scrap paper ball is well covered. Once the whole bird is wrapped, turn it over and tie the loose ends of the yarn on the back side to ensure the yarn doesn't unravel.

5. Make the wing. Trace around the cardboard wing shape on some colored paper, cut out the paper wing, and glue the paper wing to the cardboard wing. The thick cardboard adds nice depth to the yarn-covered body. Decorate the wing with anything you can find—eco-friendly glitter, stickers, lace trim, ribbon, buttons . . . use your imagination!

6. Assemble the bird. Glue the decorated wing to the bird's body. Glue the eye and the beak to the bird's head. Finish off by adding a pair of clothespins for legs. If desired, perch your birdie on a stick.

Zebra

Combining the creativity of craft, the interest of perspective, and the fun of movement, this 3D craft will be loved by kids of all ages. With his bold pattern and friendly smile, our zebra is a great addition to a safari animal school project, or a standalone activity to brighten up a rainy day.

MATERIALS

- Template (pages 92 and 93)
- Favorite coloring medium (such as paint, crayons, or paint sticks)
- Any color backing cardstock

- 2 black cardstock strips, cut wide
- Scissors
- Glue stick

Paper Folding Technique: Loop

1. Color and cut out the template. Use your favorite paints or crayons to color the zebra. Then carefully cut out all the elements from the template. Will you make him look realistic with black and white, or make him colorful like a rainbow?

2. Attach the neck and make two loops. Glue the neck to the backing cardstock, making sure you stick it at the bottom so you have enough room for the head. But don't attach the head yet! Then create the first two paper loops using a black cardstock strip cut in half.

3. Add the loops. Glue the two loops to the backing cardstock, just above the neck, with one above the other. These loops will lift the head away from the neck. Carefully glue the zebra's head onto the two loops. Make sure you don't cover the whole back of the head with glue—otherwise he might end up stuck to the background!

4. Make the third loop. Create the third loop using the entire black cardstock strip. Then gently flatten it a little between your hands, without creating a crease.

5. Add the loop. Glue the third loop onto the bottom of the zebra's head.

6. Assemble the face. Glue the ears, eyes, and tuft of hair to the upper area of the zebra's head. Finally, glue the nose onto the third paper loop. Your smiley zebra friend is ready to spring into action and bounce, wobble, and wiggle!

Templates

Photocopy all templates at 100% or at desired size.

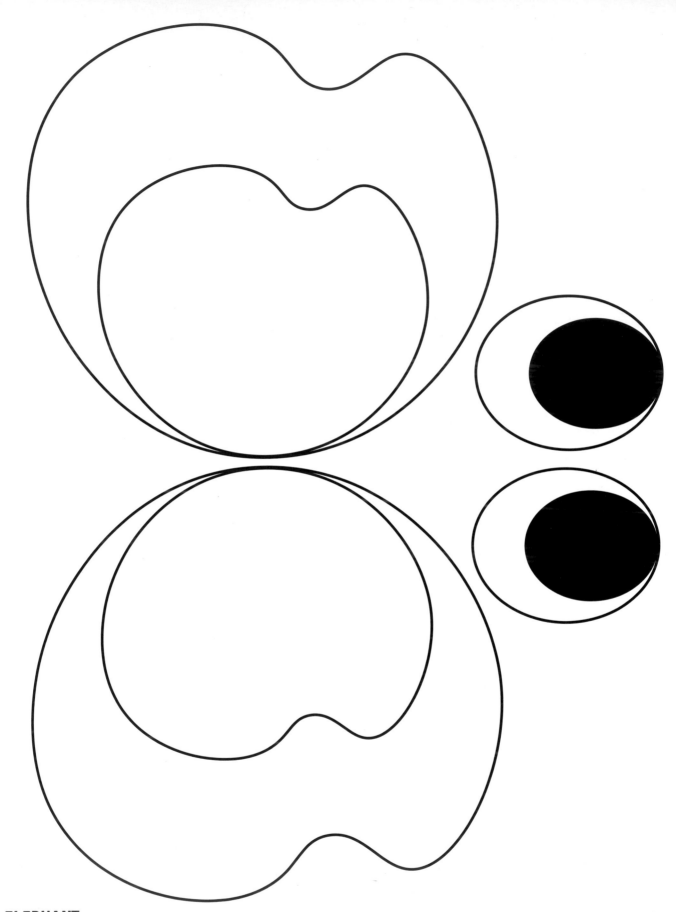

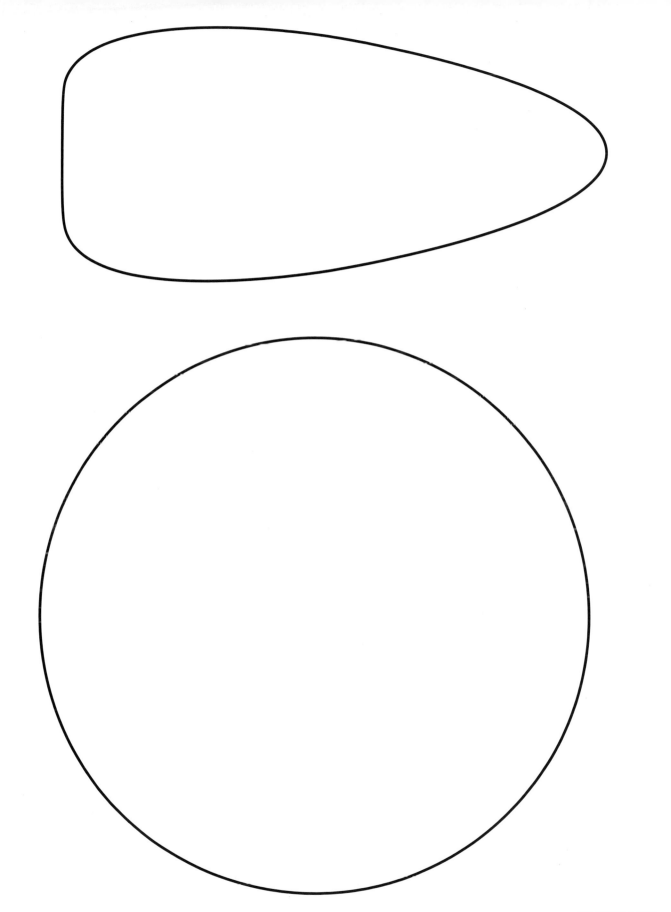

ELEPHANT 69

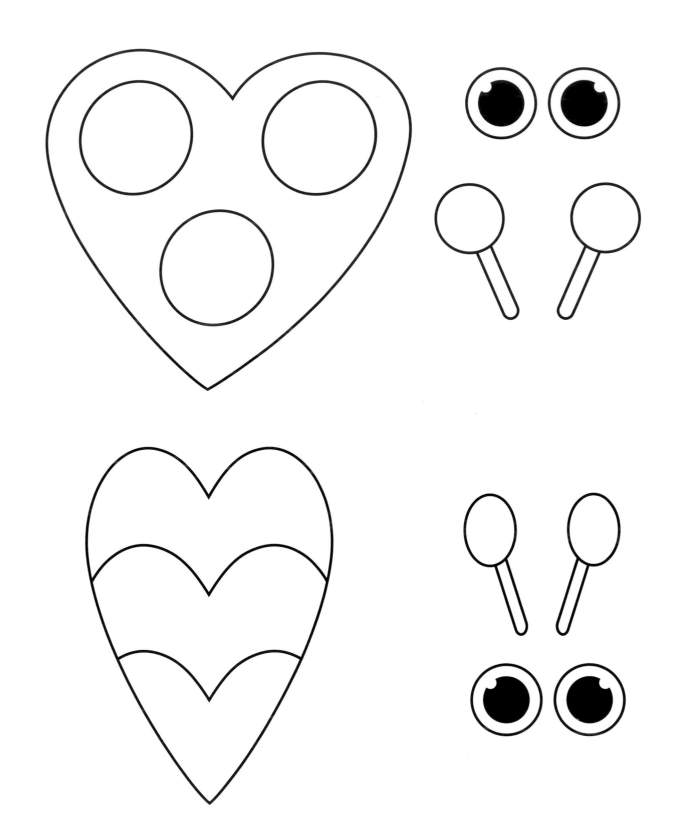

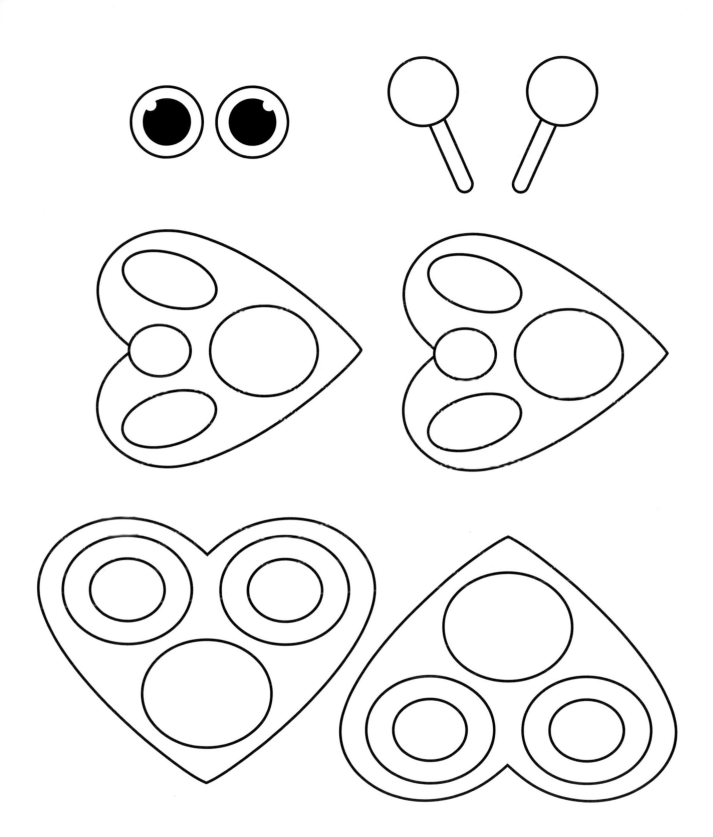

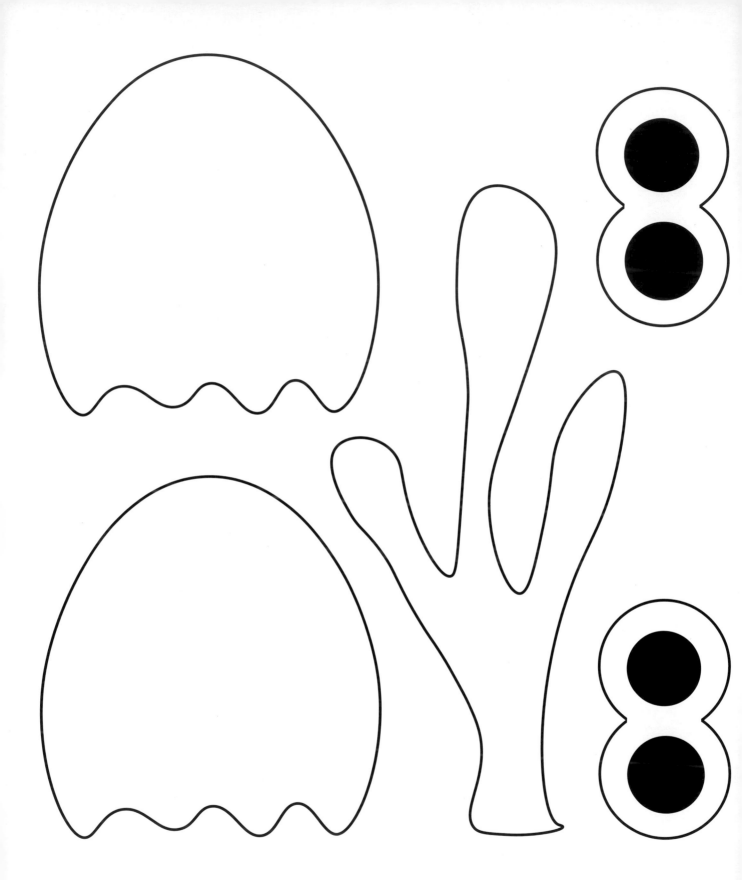

POLAR BEAR

Pattern from *3D Paper Crafts for Kids* © Helen Drew and Happy Fox Books, an imprint of Fox Chapel Publishing.

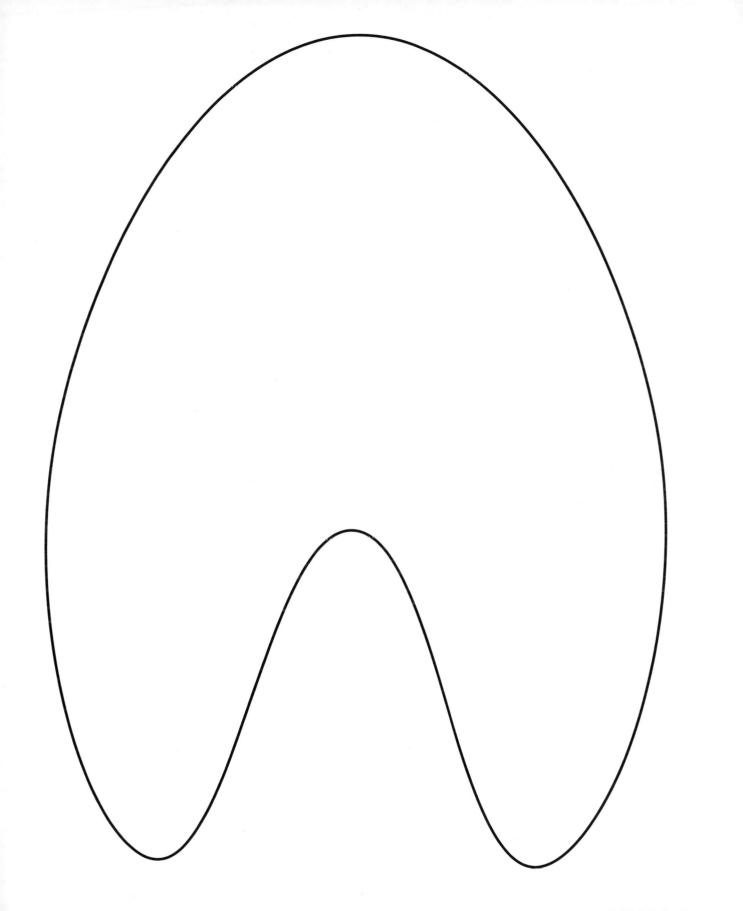

Pattern from *3D Paper Crafts for Kids* © Helen Drew and Happy Fox Books, an imprint of Fox Chapel Publishing.

POLAR BEAR 81

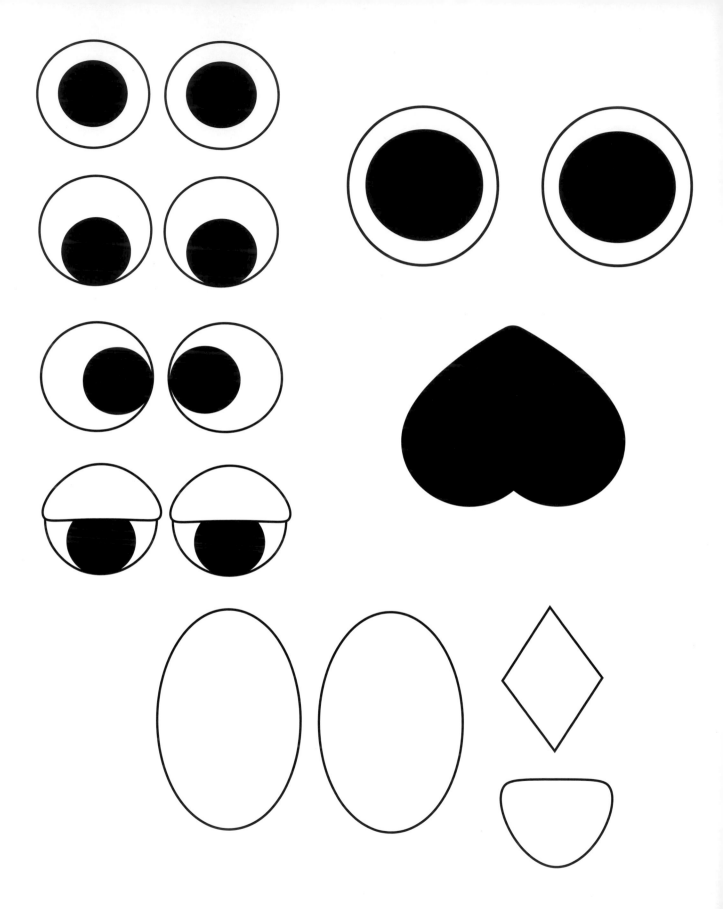

Pattern from *3D Paper Crafts for Kids* © Helen Drew and Happy Fox Books, an imprint of Fox Chapel Publishing.

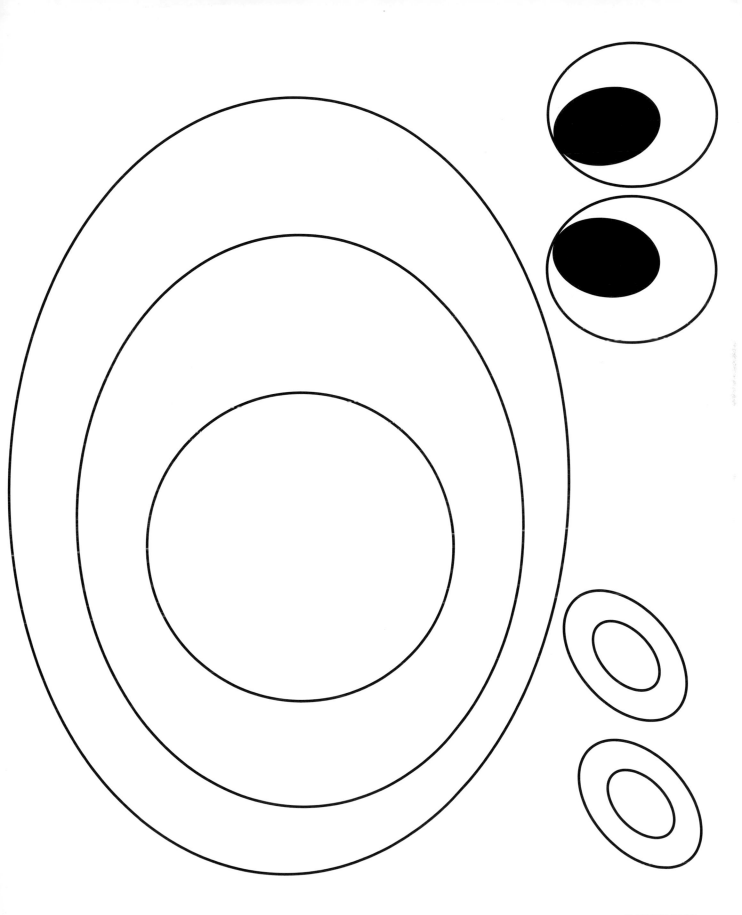

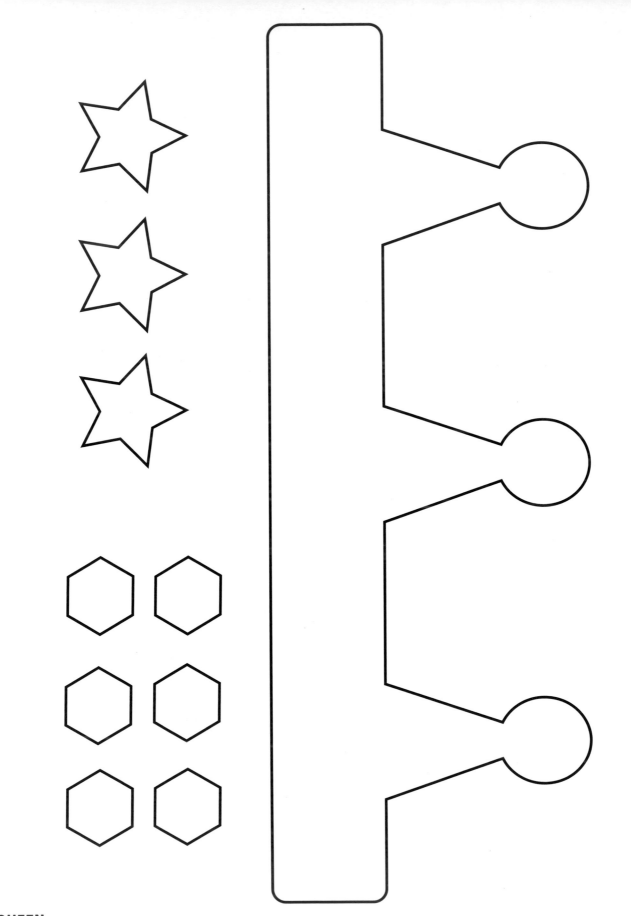

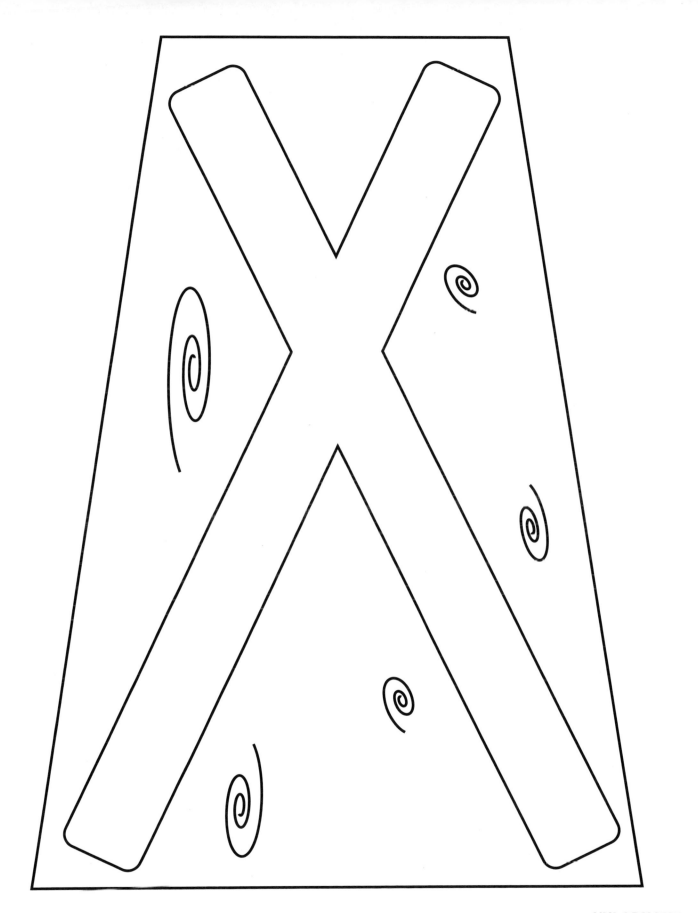

UNICORN

Pattern from *3D Paper Crafts for Kids* © Helen Drew and Happy Fox Books, an imprint of Fox Chapel Publishing.

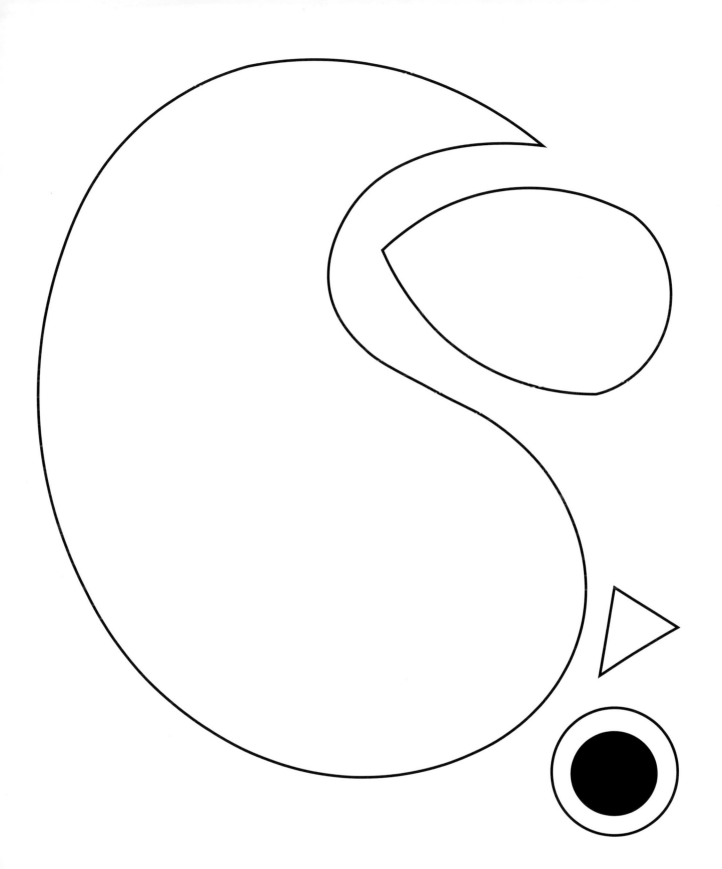

Pattern from *3D Paper Crafts for Kids* © Helen Drew and Happy Fox Books, an imprint of Fox Chapel Publishing.

94 VASE WITH FLOWER   Pattern from *3D Paper Crafts for Kids* © Helen Drew and Happy Fox Books, an imprint of Fox Chapel Publishing.

About the Author

Helen Drew is the creator and owner of Arty Crafty Kids, where she offers membership-based arts and crafts projects for children. What started as an outlet to share and document her own children's creative adventures in 2014 has grown into a community of hundreds of thousands worldwide. In today's technology-driven world, Helen's hands-on projects and craft templates aim to help children develop their creativity, confidence, problem-solving skills, fine motor skills, and more.

To see Helen's work, visit her website, *www.ArtyCraftyKids.com*, or find her on Facebook, Instagram, YouTube, and Pinterest under the handle @ArtyCraftyKids.

Acknowledgments

Firstly, I would like to thank Amelia, Kerry, Elizabeth, Colleen, and everyone at Fox Chapel Publishing for the opportunity to fulfill a lifelong dream.

My (and the original) Arty Crafty Kids—Olivia, Eden, and Dylan. Pigeons, rainbows, and monster trucks will forever be a source of inspiration for my creativity. I love you.

My partner in life, John. Thank you for being you, and for all of the support you have given me in turning this book into a reality.

Jo and Fiona, thank you for your continued support with Arty Crafty Kids, your friendship, and your contributions to this book—you're both amazing!

And I would like to extend my heartfelt gratitude to each and every person across the world who has used Arty Crafty Kids as a source of inspiration and creativity.

Index

Note: Page numbers in (parentheses) indicate project templates.